A Case for the Capacity of South Sudanese to Rule Themselves

Akol Miyen Kuol

Akol Miyen Kuol

A Case for the Capacity of South Sudanese to Rule Themselves

A CASE FOR THE CAPACITY OF SOUTH SUDANESE TO RULE THEMSELVES

First published in 2009 by
Akol Miyen Kuol
Nairobi, Kenya

ISBN-13: 978-1495993862
ISBN-10: 1495993868

CONTENTS

DEDICATION

This book is dedicated to my colleague and friend, the late poet Joseph Ater Dhieu who was from Rumbek, South Sudan and who recited a poem in our secondary school in 1992, in which he urged South Sudanese to unite. I am also dedicating it to Nhial Deng Nhial who is my role model in journalism and the late Mario Muor Muor for encouraging me to carry on with writing.

ABOUT THE AUTHOR

*T*he author and poet, Akol Miyen Kuol, commonly known as Akoldit was born in 1974 in Thurkuruk village in the water and oil-rich region of Abyei. Due to the continuous political instability in Abyei, he deserted the region in 1978 and underwent studies in Khartoum and Al-Jazirah State, Sudan.

He left Sudan in January 1993 and has since lived in exile until the country split into two in 2011. In 1997, the author was secretary-general of the Abyei community in Egypt. From 2000 to 2001, he worked with UNICEF/Operation Lifeline Sudan on Life Skills Educational Programmes for South Sudan.

He co-authored a booklet for UNICEF entitled, 'Life Skills Programme for South Sudan, HIV and AIDS, Information and Activity Book for Mentors', 2001. Akol was a contributor to the Sudan Mirror newspaper from 2004 to 2007 and was one of its columnists. His column was entitled 'The Sun Will be Rising' in a page titled 'Focus on Abyei'.

In 2006, he worked with the National Democratic Institute for International Affairs (NDI) on the implementation of the Sudan's Comprehensive Peace Agreement. From 2001 to 2005, he was a regular contributor to the BBC on Sudanese, African and world issues. Akol's poems have been aired over the BBC World Service and Sudan Radio Service on several occasions.

The author has published two collections of poems titled 'The Sun Will be Rising', 2001 and 'The Last Train', 2003, as well as an analytical book entitled, 'Sudan: Understanding the Oil-Rich Region of Abyei', 2011.

He also published a paper in 1997 in Cairo, Egypt entitled 'The Obstacles of Creativity in South Sudan', in which he proposed among other recommendations, a confederation system as a solution to Sudan and South Sudan problem.

Akol is married to Christine Nyanakol Gordon Riak with whom he has three children, Mijak, Nyenawut and Kuol (Mandela).

A Case for the Capacity of South Sudanese to Rule Themselves was first published in 2009, two years ahead of Southern Sudan Referendum. The book is a collection of articles which I wrote and published in the Sudan Mirror newspaper between 2004 and 2007.

The purpose of writing and publishing the articles was to pave the way for the people of South Sudan, the SPLM/A, other political parties, religious and armed groups, as well as the civil society organizations, to embark on a comprehensive reconciliation and healing programme upon the signing of the Comprehensive Peace Agreement (CPA).

However, that was not the case instead all the stakeholders including the ruling SPLM with its government, which should have spearheaded the healing process did not consider it to be a priority during and after the six-year interim period. Hence this failure led to the fighting that broke out in Juba on 15 December 2013 between members of the Presidential Guards of Tiger Battalion who hail from the Dinka and Nuer ethnic groups.

The five-week old violence has led to the death of over 1,000 people and displaced over 470,000 according to the UN, while the International Crisis Group says 10,000 have been killed and half a million people have taken refuge in neighbouring countries.

As a matter of fact, the Juba violence, which spread very fast like a wild fire to Jonglei, Unity and Upper Nile states was a power struggle between members of the SPLM, which easily found its way to the national army due to the lack of well established institutions and ideology in the world's youngest nation, and that is why leaders from this part of the world resort to their ethnic groups on such occasions to get support.

However, the two groups within the SPLM/A must understand that violence is not the best way for resolving their differences. The infighting within the SPLM/A which started on 15 December 2013 had raised more questions than answers. Hence one wonders, if members of the same ruling party cannot stand each other, how will they coexist and work together with the rest of South Sudanese political parties, civil society organizations, individuals, religious and human rights groups?!

Moreover, the infighting within South Sudan has left the Ngok Dinka people of Abyei, who conducted their long-awaited referendum in October 2013 in accordance with the timeframe set by the African Union High-Level Implementation Panel Proposal on the Final Status of Abyei Area, wondering about the future of their region. Neither Sudan nor South Sudan has recognized the outcome of the plebiscite. The nine Ngok Dinka Chiefdoms of Abyei chose during the "unrecognized" referendum to join South Sudan.

The future status of the Ngok Dinka and their homeland, Abyei, is in a dilemma once more as their fellow South Sudanese are fighting each other, risking the existence of their newly-born country and the hard-won independence and freedom. The infighting within the SPLM/A has put the future of the country and Abyei region at stake.

Therefore, the two warring parties should stop fighting each other militarily and over the media immediately and unconditionally and embark on a serious national reconciliation and healing process without further delays. They must work on a political settlement to iron out their differences and pave the way for all South Sudanese national conference as soon as possible.

Holding a national constitutional conference that will be attended by the national stakeholders and backed by South Sudan friends and allies, is paramount as it is through an inclusive conference where a permanent constitution that will clearly spell out the rights, duties, obligations and responsibilities of individuals, governments and institutions can be made.

It is advisable for South Sudanese people to choose the path of peace as they have already suffered enough. South Sudanese leaders need to put the interests of the public ahead of self-or narrow political parties' interests.

In conclusion, I appeal to the international community, especially the permanent members of the United Nations Security Council and the African Union Peace and Security Council as well as the Inter-Governmental Authority on Development (IGAD) to continue standing with the people of South Sudan including the Ngok Dinka people of Abyei at this trying time until they realize a durable peace, justice, freedom, stability and prosperity.

Akol Miyen Kuol
20 January 2014
Nairobi, Kenya

PREFACE

Sudan became independent from the British on 1 January, 1956. It is the largest country in Africa, occupying an area nearly one million square miles. Sudan is as big as the United Kingdom, France, Italy and the Scandinavian countries combined. Muslims make up 70% of the population while Christians and those who believe in African traditional religions make up 30%. Blacks, Muslims, Christians and believers of African religions comprise 52% of the populace while 39% are Arabs. Hamitic people such as the Beja in the east constitute 9% of the population.

Our country has about 597 tribes and sub-tribes, which broadly comprise 56 major tribal groups. The population growth is 2.2% per annum with a life expectancy of 54 years and child mortality rate of 77 per 1000 live births according to 1995 statistics (Suffering and God: A Theological Reflection on the War in Sudan).

The current population of Sudan is estimated to be 39 million people according to the outcome of the Fifth National Population Census of 2008. According to Dr Luka Biong Deng, Minister of Presidential Affairs of the Government of Southern Sudan, the population of Southern Sudan is approximately between 12 and 13 million people (Luka Biong Deng, 2003).

The Comprehensive Peace Agreement [CPA], has given hope of a stable, just, peaceful and democratic new Sudan. However, the non-implementation of some provisions of the CPA will deepen the existing lack of trust between the north and south, something that threatens the unity of the country.

The vision of the SPLM/A since its inception in 1983 has been a just, secular, democratic and united new Sudan. However, this has never been welcomed by central governments in Khartoum.

Following a split in the SPLM/A in 1991, the movement held the Chukudum Convention in Eastern Equatoria, South Sudan to reorganize itself. The convention came up with a number of resolutions; among them the one which declared: "the New Sudan for the time being, shall consist of Bahr al-Ghazal, Equatoria, Southern Blue Nile, Southern Kordufan and Upper Nile regions as proclaimed by the First National Convention of the SPLM in 1994" (Peace Through Development in Sudan, January 2000).

Politically, Sudan is divided into two regions; north and south. Darfur, west, central and eastern Sudan are part of the north. On 9 January 2011, the people of Southern Sudan will vote at a referendum to decide whether they want to remain part of a united Sudan or secede and set up their own country. People of the Abyei region will also decide on the same date if they want to remain part of the north or rejoin Southern Sudan.

Those in the two contested areas of the Nuba Mountains and Southern Blue Nile which are politically, geographically, and administratively considered parts of the north were to decide their future at the end of the fourth year of the interim period through a popular consultation within their two parliaments [Southern Kordufan and Blue Nile states]. Unfortunately the fourth year passed without the popular consultation being conducted. This will now happen after the general elections of 2010.

It is preferable for the country to remain united, secular, peaceful and democratic, with equal opportunities for all. However, in the absence of these, the outcome may lead to the creation of a new Sudan made up of the south, including Abyei, Nuba Mountains, Southern Blue Nile, Eastern Sudan and Darfur region. OR Darfur region may decide its own fate and opt for an independent state, same as the East. OR the Nuba Mountains and Southern Blue Nile may opt to remain part of the south and form the Republic of New Sudan. Another possibility is that the two regions may opt not to join the south; in which case the new state will be the Republic of South Sudan.

Though Southern Sudanese have the right to a state of their own, it would be a landlocked country since the region will lose Port Sudan. Thus, they will have difficulties importing goods. Moreover, a separate South Sudan will have hard times for sometimes as far as tribalism is concerned. 'A Case for the Capacity of South Sudanese to Rule Themselves' is a collection of articles which I wrote and published in the Sudan Mirror newspaper between 2004 and 2007.

Akol Miyen Kuol
October 2009
Nairobi, Kenya

FOREWORD

Sudan: A country in need of Peace Heroes

"During war time we had/have war heroes. As we go to peace now, we will also need to have peace heroes."

The words from the author of this book, Akol Miyen Kuol (commonly known as Akoldit) is a real challenge to a war-torn society living inside as well as outside of its home country, Sudan. For a life time of over 50 years wars and civil conflicts have been the sad story of a beautiful and rich country, a country once known as the 'food chamber' of Africa and still rich on mineral resources like petroleum, natural gas, gold, silver, chrome, asbestos, manganese, gypsum, mica, zinc, iron, lead, uranium, copper, kaolin, cobalt, granite, nickel and tin.

The facts about Sudan (as found online at wikipedia.org) tell a very sad story. It is a story that needs a new generation to fill the future with hope and creativity! And Akoldit points to the role of poetry and songs as natural paths of healing for his people. But first we need to reiterate the sad story in order to learn and gain strength and resolution to develop a new and better future:

Sudan is home to one of the world's oldest continuous major civilizations, with historical and urban settlements dating back to 3000 BC. The people of Sudan have a long history extending from antiquity, which is intertwined with the history of Egypt, with which it was united politically over several periods. After gaining independence from the United Kingdom in 1956, Sudan suffered a civil war, lasting 17 years. In 1955, the year before independence, a civil war began between Northern and Southern Sudan. The southerners, anticipating independence, feared the new nation would be dominated by the north. Historically, the north of Sudan had closer ties with Egypt and was predominantly Arab and Muslim (an estimated 70% of the population adheres to Islam) while the south was predominantly a mixture of Christianity (25%) and Animism (5%). The 1955 war began when Southern army officers mutinied and then formed the Anya-Nya guerilla movement.

In 1972, a cessation of the north-south conflict was agreed upon under the terms of the Addis Ababa Agreement, following talks which were sponsored by the World Council of Churches. This led to a ten-year hiatus in the national conflict.

In 1983, the civil war was reignited following President Ja'far Numayri's decision to circumvent the Addis Ababa Agreement. PresidentJa'far Numayri attempted to create a federated Sudan including states in southern Sudan, which violated the Addis Ababa Agreement that had granted the south considerable autonomy. The Sudan People's Liberation Army (SPLA), based in southern Sudan, was formed in May 1983. The war went on for more than 20 years, including the use of Russian-made combat helicopters and military cargo planes which were used as bombers to devastating effect on villages and tribal rebels alike. "Sudan's independent history has been dominated by chronic, exceptionally cruel warfare that has starkly divided the country on racial, religious, and regional grounds; displaced an estimated four million people (of a total estimated population of thirty-two million); and killed an estimated two million people." (end note)
It damaged Sudan's economy and led to food shortages, resulting in starvation and malnutrition. The lack of investment during this time, particularly in the south, meant a generation lost access to basic health services, education, and jobs.

Peace talks between the southern rebels and the government made substantial progress in 2003 and early 2004. The peace was consolidated with the official signing by both sides of the Nairobi

Comprehensive Peace Agreement 9 January 2005, granting Southern Sudan autonomy for six years, to be followed by a referendum about independence. It created a co-vice president position and allowed the north and south to split oil deposits equally, but also left both the north's and south's armies in place. John Garang, the south's peace agreement appointed co-vice president died in a (suspicious) helicopter crash on 1 August [30 July] 2005, three weeks after being sworn in. This resulted in riots, but the peace was eventually able to continue.

Due to significant cultural, social, political, ethnic and economic changes in short amounts of time, conflicts evolved in western and eastern provinces of Sudan in addition to an escalating conflict in Southern Sudan. Even since the 2005 CPA several violent struggles between the Janjaweed militia and rebel groups such as the Sudan Liberation Movement (SLM), Sudanese Liberation Army (SLA) and the Justice and Equality Movement (JEM) has resulted in death tolls between 200,000 - 400,000, and over 2.5 million people being displaced. A cruel and costly peace!

The story of civil war in Sudan has international ramifications: On 4 March 2009, the International Criminal Court (ICC) issued an arrest warrant for President Umar al-Bashir on charges of war crimes and crimes against humanity, the first sitting head of state ever indicted by the ICC.

If these facts are not enough, Sudan still has yet another sad story to tell of slavery in modern times. Slavery has been documented since Egypt was taken over by the Ottoman Empire and the subsequent institutionalizing of Shar'iah law in the north. The amount of war prisoners being forced into slavery increased significantly during and after the Second Sudanese Civil War, as Umar al-Bashir seized power in 1989 and created a totalitarian federal government supporting Arab militias terrorizing the southern regions, such as raiding non-Afro Arab villages and looting them both for property and for slaves. *Since 1995, international rights organizations such as Human Rights Watch have reported that slavery in Sudan is a common fate of captives in the Second Sudanese Civil War.

Thus Sudan faces tremendous challenges for the future. Despite being the 17th fastest growing economy in the world with new economic policies and infrastructure investments, Sudan still has formidable economic problems, as it must rise from a very low level of per capita output.

So, Akoldit is right: *As we go to peace now, we will also need to have peace heroes.*

Upcoming elections need peace heroes to lead the way. Abyei is to hold a referendum in 2011 on whether to join South Sudan or not. Southern Sudan is scheduled to have a referendum on independence in 2011. These issues cry out for a strong and resolute people with trusted leaders with a common goal to establish a real peace in mind. The genuine challenge, according to Akoldit is: *"The present/future of South Sudan is in our hands and we can shape it the way we want for the betterment and well-being of our people who have been suffering throughout their lives. If the Southerners remain united during the Interim Period, and they must, they will be strong and therefore change the direction of Sudan for the better."*

The first challenge is to make a mutual agreement on a common foundation and basis: *"We all know that Sudan is a multi-racial, multi-cultural, multi-religious, multi-lingual and multi-ethnic, and if at all there is going to be unity, it should be unity in diversity and not by imposing one of these on the rest."* Only with such an agreement can peace be built for the future – even if the final result is two separate states.

The second challenge is to gain strength through using the old, good tools of poetry and songs. *"Our history has been carried on from one generation to the next through songs"* writes Akoldit. And this book gives many examples of poetry and men and women writing to heal people's minds and hearts by poetry.

My own very tiny part in the history of Southern Sudan started back in the middle of the short-lived peace period between the two civil wars. As a young boy in high school in my home country,

Norway, and member of the National Board of the High School Students Union I was looking around to find a good project for our annual "Give A Day" campaign. A friend from church working with the Norwegian Church Aid suggested their new project to build higher educational schools in Juba and Torit in Southern Sudan.

I agreed and started my own (self-financed) campaign to promote the project. As I arrived at the National Convention later in the year of 1976 I was surprised to discover that my project had won a majority of the votes in elections around the country – a real God-incidental result. The following year more than USD 350,000 was collected and the schools built in due time. But I am sure the next civil war that followed in 1983 crushed the buildings to the ground . . .

The third challenge is to build a culture of creativity. As Akoldit writes, *"It is time now we show the world that we are also creative people. Much of our talents have not yet been discovered and therefore not exploited. Our oral literature has not yet been documented. . . . It is through creativity only that we will put back Sudan in general and Southern Sudan in particular on the map of the world as a full active member of the international community."* The challenges to build a better education for all people, and new media in the South to nurture and promote expressions of life, faith and hope and foster a new peace culture are very clear and strong. A small sign that this may be possible can be found in the fact that Southern Sudan has one of the fastest growing Christian populations (Roman Catholic, Anglican and Coptic Orthodox) in the whole world; new churches in the South are being built very frequently.

But can and will peace come to the still suffering people in war-torn Southern Sudan? At this point in history we do not know. Still, all people of peace and good will inside as well as outside of Sudan need to unite in work (and prayers) for this to happen.

Rev. Dr. Arne H. Fjeldstad
CEO, The Media Project

(End note) * Morrison, J. Stephen and Alex de Waal. "Can Sudan Escape its Intractability?" **Grasping the Nettle: Analyzing Cases of Intractable Conflict**. Eds. Crocker, Chester A., Fen Osler Hampson, and Pamel Aall. Washington, D.C.: United States Institute of Peace, 2005, p. 162.

"Today, writers are the ones best equipped to create and communicate the synthesis of ideas needed to solve the present predicaments, the world over. They should continue (as peace-lovers) to articulate their imaginative and prophetic visions."

Nigerian writer Yemi D. Ogunyemi

SONGS AND LIBERATION STRUGGLES IN ABYEI

Sudan Mirror newspaper, September 20th-October 3rd, 2004

The history of the Ngok Dinka of Abyei has been that of liberation, protection and preservation of their culture and values.

The real massive displacement of the Ngok Dinka people of Abyei started in 1965, when the Missiriyah Arab tribe massacred and burned around 200 Abyei people in Mujled locality in the Abyei region, and Babanusa town in Kordufan, western Sudan, and the bloody battle between the Missiriyah and the Ngok people in Ngol-Kou River, north-east of the Abyei region, led to the massive displacement that has continued up to the present time.

Most of the Ngok Dinka people of Abyei are in northern towns of Sudan, and some are in South Sudan and thousands others are in Diaspora. They are made up of nine tribal sections or nine chiefdoms, namely: Abior, Achaak, Achueng, Allei, Anyel, Bongo, Diil, Man-nyuar and Mareng.

Despite this long and massive displacement in northern Sudan, the Ngok Dinka people of Abyei have managed to preserve their values, language and culture. They are known for their love for singing. It is to be-recalled that Abyei region was transferred by the British in 1905 from Bahr Al-Ghazal Province in South Sudan to Kordufan Province in northern Sudan.

The Ngok Dinka people of Abyei are gifted in music; and the Abyei singers have been playing a very instrumental role in their struggle, and in fact, their songs have been one of the sources of strength, unity and determination for the Ngok

Dinka to continue the struggle for the liberation of their homeland, and preservation of their culture.

The population of the Ngok Dinka of Abyei is approximately 300,000 people and the size of the Abyei region is around 30,000 square kilo meters.

The current population in the Abyei Area is estimated to be 45,000 people. The Ngok Dinka people of Abyei are part of the Dinka Padaang whose majority of them reside in Upper Nile Region, which is now one of the ten states of South Sudan.

Other parts of the Padaang Dinka are Pan-Arou, Dongjol, Ngok Lual Yak, Nyarweng, Ahoal, Ageer, Alor (Ruweng), Abaliang, Paweny, Luach, Nyiel, Thoi and Rud. There is a small number of Padaang in Bahr Al-Ghazal Region. They are Luach and Kuach. It is 50 years now (1954-2004) since the Ngok Dinka people of Abyei started their struggle.

The British started leaving Sudan since 1953 and with Sudanisation, the educated Ngok of Abyei and officials in the area were transferred to South Sudan and replaced with the

Arab officials who undertook the Islamisation and Arabisation of the Ngok Dinka.

In 1954, an Ngok student movement made consultations with the nine chiefs of the nine chiefdoms of the Ngok Dinka of Abyei, including their then Paramount Chief, Deng Kuol Arob, who was generally known as Deng Majok.

The students were demanding the return of their homeland, Abyei to South Sudan and they got the full support of the Ngok people. They, therefore, formed a delegation of the educated youth who were sent to Rijl al-Fullah town in Kordufan, to convey the message but they were arrested by the authorities in Kordufan Province.

They later joined the southern rebellion which began on 18 August 1955 in an army garrison in Torit town [capital of Eastern Equatoria State], South Sudan. The Ngok Dinka people were simply denied the right to exercise the option given to them by the British within five years to decide their fate between remaining part of the north or restore their homeland to southern Sudan.

Since the Arabisation of the education system in Abyei in 1953, no Ngok student was admitted to intermediate [junior school] till 1967. As a result of these discriminatory practices the people of Abyei joined southern rebellion in 1955, especially the educated youth who came back from Egypt. They were dismissed from the Egyptian universities because of their stand against the alleged unity between Egypt and Sudan.

One of the prominent leaders of the Ngok Dinka in Anyanya I [first southern liberation movement/army] was Akonon e Mithiang. Throughout these years the Ngok Dinka people of Abyei have been using various means of the struggle, including songs, to liberate their homeland, Abyei.

I remember one of the prominent singers called Ajing e Bulabek, who is one of the Ngok Dinka people of Abyei displaced to the north. He composed a very beautiful song about a girlfriend who was about to go back to Abyei. In the song, the listener can sense the mixture of feelings of love of the singer for his girlfriend, Adau, and his homeland, Abyei. Here are the lyrics:

Adau nyan wun e Bongo,

Adau nyan wun e Bongo,

Akol bin la bei,

Akol bin la bei,

Ka yin baar e yien Abyein dan e Ngok,

Ka yin baar e yien Abyein dan e Ngok,

Did den nyieng piny,

Yen bi nyin lek ngong

Yen bi nyin lek kuany.

It translates:

Adau, the girl from Bongo Chiefdom,

Adau, the girl from Bongo Chiefdom.

When you go home,

When you go home,

Please, take me with you to our Abyei of Ngok,

Please, take me with you to our Abyei of Ngok.

Do not leave me behind,

Because I will be feeling lonely,

Because I will be feeling sad.

Ajing e Bulabek has been singing since the Ngok Dinka people of Abyei were displaced by the Missiriyah from Ngol-Kou River (Highland) in 1965. A'ishah Mithiang also appeared in the 1960s; however, she stopped singing in the 1970s when she got married.

Somebody like Nyankol e Mithiang Dut appreaed in the first half of the 1970s and she is still singing up to now. Most of her songs are about the struggle of the black people in Sudan, the love of the Ngok Dinka people of Abyei for their homeland, Abyei, equality, justice and the persistence of the African culture. She released an album in 2002 in Canada. It is entitled *'Dot Ku Baai'*, which means *'Let us rescue the homeland'*. It also translates *'Let us rescue the country'*.

Another Abyei band, called *Shabab Abyei*, which means in English 'Abyei Youth', released an album in 2002 entitled *'Arong ke Yien'* which means *'She suits me'*. The songs are mixed with romance and love for Abyei. They also call on the sons and daughters of Abyei to go back to Abyeiland. Another singer who has more than 30 years in singing is Marco Kuol Diing. He has released an album recently, entitled *'Ajel e Guuk'* which translates 'Dove-let'. In this album, Kuol also calls on the Ngok Dinka people of Abyei to go back to their homeland.

Earlier on this year, the only well organized musical band in the areas controlled by the SPLM/A called *Abyei Jazz Band*, released an album entitled, *'Bar Welki'* which means 'Deliver my message'.

These are the lyrics of the song *'Bar Welki'*:

Tingen da, yien achol ku bar,

Ku luoi kak e Monyjang ke loi,

Ke e raan en yok yien ache Monyjang.

Bar welki, lor e chol Abyei Jazz,

Bar e kek yiin Ngok atuung diak.

It translates:

Look at me; I am black and tall,

And I do what the Dinka do,

Despite all this, somebody is telling me

That I am not a Dinka.

Deliver my message, you Abyei Jazz Band,

Deliver it, you Ngok of three horns.

Here *Abyei Jazz Band* is trying to question those who say that the Ngok Dinka people of Abyei are not Dinka and are not South Sudanese, it asks: how can the Ngok Dinka of Abyei be denied their identity of being Dinka even when they are black, tall, speak the Dinka Language and even have the Dinka culture?

One of the greatest revolutionary singers of the Ngok Dinka of Abyei was *Deng e Mithiang*. He was nicknamed '*Deng RPG*'. He was one of the fighters of the Jamuus Battalion [Buffalo Battalion] in the SPLA.

He sang about the Abyei crisis, the destruction of Abyei and how the people and cattle were killed/ abducted by the Missiriyah Arab tribesmen and how he had to leave the land to go and look for power and come back to liberate Abyei and rescue his people. Unfortunately, he lost his life in the armed struggle before he could see the fate of the Abyeiland and the Ngok Dinka people of Abyei.

Recently one of the young musicians from Abyei called Teng e Ma'ngok released an album entitled *'Juju'*.

Other singers of the Ngok Dinka of Abyei are Mi'nyiel e Noon, Chol e Mabil, Amir e Deng, Agok Dau, to mention but a few. It is because of these musicians and others whom I did not mention that the revolutionary spirit of the Ngok Dinka people of Abyei is always flaming.

They all believe in the unity of the people and land. They will still inspire the Ngok Dinka people of Abyei during the six-year interim period to unite, work hard and remain focused so that they restore their beloved homeland, Abyei, upon the end of the interim period to South Sudan when the Ngok Dinka of Abyei's ancestors lived as part and parcel of the Dinka community.

Even amid the political controversies surrounding Abyei and the Ngok Dinka of Abyei, music has continued to inspire the spirit of togetherness and love for their culture. The Ngok continue to express their suffering, inspirations and culture in the form of music.

WE SHOULD NOT WATCH OUR

LANGUAGES

Sudan Mirror newspaper-October 4th-October17th, 2004

Whenever we want to talk about social, agricultural and economic development, our thoughts usually dwell on the effect of war on these aspects. There is no doubt that the long and destructive two civil wars, have in most cases, affected South Sudan and South Sudanese negatively.

P eople always go to war for many reasons. Some are economic and social and others are political. South Sudanese and people of the three conflict areas of the Nuba Mountains, Southern Blue Nile and Abyei went to war because of these reasons I mentioned above and others.

Now after 21-year civil war, there are mounting hopes that peace might come, especially, after the two parties signed the Machakos Protocol on 20 July 2002, which grants South Sudan the right to self-determination after a six-year interim period, whether to remain in one united Sudan or secede, Security Arrangements Protocol on 25 September 2003, Wealth-Sharing Protocol on 7 January 2004, the Resolution on the Abyei Conflict on 26 May 2004, Power-Sharing Protocol on 26 May 2004, and the Resolution of the Conflict in the Two States of Southern Kordufan and Southern Blue Nile on 26 May 2004.

No matter how long it is going to take, peace will be achieved and people will embark on development. In fact, my major concern here is the future of our languages. They are in danger, especially with this age of globalization, unless something is done to preserve them.

European countries were groups of tribes with different languages and dialects but with time some of these languages and dialects disappeared. A language is one of the tools through which the culture or history of a given nation/country can be preserved or documented. Most of our languages are not written.

And the written ones are not being developed into scientific languages so that they absorb scientific development. Our history has been carried on from one generation to the next through songs. Many of us have been away for so long from the environment where these languages and dialects are spoken.

We will have a problem with the children who are born outside their homes of origin. For the necessity of a language, some people around the world are still struggling to preserve and develop their languages. For example the Barber people in Algeria have been fighting for years and years to preserve their culture and language and make it an official language. Eventually, after a long struggle and persistence, it has been recognized by the Algerian government to be an official language. This is apart from French and Arabic languages.

Also, in the United Kingdom, the people of Wales are still preserving their language and they have what they call the

'Language Council'. In countries where there are so many languages like Sudan, it is sometimes hard to select an official language or a language of instruction.

Some countries tried to solve the issue of an official language/ language of instruction and faced difficulties. One of the countries that tried to solve this matter and failed was the former Soviet Union which was made up of 183 nationalities. They chose the language of the smallest nationality- that is Russia- to be the national language. But maybe this attempt failed because of the ideology of communism.

One of my main concerns when I was in Tanzania some years back was how the first Tanzanian president, the late Mwalimu Julius Nyerere, managed to tackle the issue of the official language for a country made up of 125 tribes and how he managed to solve the problem of tribalism. I later on realized that he introduced Kiswahili as the official language and English the second language.

I also got a chance to visit the Republic of South Africa in 1997, when the firstly-elected democratic government came to power under the former president Nelson Mandela. I found out that the rainbow government had recognized all the 11 languages as official.

Kenya has made English and Kiswahili as the mediums of instructions in the government and public institutions. There are 42 tribes with 42 languages and dialects in Kenya. The concerned people of these languages have worked hard to develop and preserve them.

For example, Kikuyu tribe has made practical steps towards preservation and development of its language, it has a radio FM and some of the sons and daughters of the tribe write books in Kikuyu, one of them is the renowned Kenyan writer Ngugi wa Thiong'o who has written a number of novels in his mother tongue.

With these few examples and with the experience of the people of the new Sudan, perhaps we will be obliged to try to answer or address these issues, because these are some of the challenges awaiting us. Of course, one of the reasons we fought this war is because we want to preserve and protect our customs, traditions, cultures, values and languages.

Therefore, it would be worth for the government of the new Sudan and the masters of languages to be very careful when addressing the issues of the official language on the one hand, and how the local languages can be developed and preserved.

It could be logical if the English language is adopted as the official language and a language of instruction in the five regions of the new Sudan, and of course Arabic language has imposed itself as a language of the market, therefore there is a need for teaching it in schools as one of the foreign languages from primary to secondary schools. Meanwhile, our languages should all be recognized as official and should be embodied in the national constitution.

Children have the capacity to learn three languages at least at the same time; therefore, there is a possibility for our children from all the five regions of New Sudan of speaking at least three languages (Mother-tongue, English and Arabic) fluently. Also, learning the languages of others will narrow the gaps between our tribes, hence, minimizing the problem of tribalism.

When the [late] chairman and commander-in- chief of the SPLM/A, Dr John Garang, visited Abyei on 16 June 2004, to explain the peace protocols, the Ngok Dinka people of Abyei were astonished and extremely happy when Commander Pa'gan Amum [who hails from from the Shilluk community] stood up and addressed them in their Ngok Dinka Language. His message was directly and fully taken. These are some of the positive things we need to do to build bridges of communications and good relations among ourselves. In Switzerland for example, children there speak at least three languages (French, German and English) fluently.

I was surprised when I was in secondary school some years back in Al-Shaykh Lutfi National Secondary School in Rufa'ah, Al-Jazirah State, Sudan, when I found a number of my colleagues from Upper Nile region [State], South Sudan, speaking around four languages (Nuer, Shilluk, Anyuak and Dinka).

This is a positive aspect and it should be encouraged. It will be important for the government of the new Sudan to assist financially in the process of developing and preserving our languages. However, the bigger responsibility will lie on the shoulders of the speakers of the language.

Local languages should be introduced to schools probably up to grade three. Cultural centres should be established for the development and promotion of these languages. Books should be written in these languages (novels, plays, poetry, and short stories).

By doing so, we would be documenting and preserving our languages, heritage and cultures. Also, there is a need for mobile theatres. Establishment of magazines and newspapers is important. Establishment of FM radios can also help preserve our culture.

With technology and the flow of information, many unwritten languages are, without doubt going to disappear within this century. So your language will have two choices, it either survives or disappears.

CREATIVITY IS STILL PART OF

SUDANESE

Sudan Mirror newspaper-October 18th-October 31st, 2004

As the country heads towards peace, what is the dearest wish of all the Sudanese people? Each and every one of us should start asking himself/herself about what he/she is going to do when the CPA is signed and peace achieved.

Some must have set their own plans/programmes already. And this is where the necessity of creativity comes in. Some may wonder what creativity is. Creativity is simply the use of talent, skill and imagination to produce something, for example (poetry, novel and plays).

Again these two long civil wars have taken 38 years of our country's progress, have undermined the creativity of the Sudanese people, especially the people of South Sudan, Abyei, Southern Blue Nile, and the Nuba Mountains. All these years, our people have been fighting just for survival since their homeland has been a theatre of war. Many of them lost the chance for education.

Natural talent is a gift from God and it should be appreciated for the benefit of society. When discovered it must be nurtured, developed and exploited up to the maximum for the benefit of oneself, the nation and human society at large. We have well-educated and knowledgeable people and they should try their best to use this knowledge and education for the development, unity and progress of our people.

Knowledge is meaningless if it is not applied productively for the betterment of human life. Some people have little education but because they are determined to achieve and make a success of their lives, they perform wonders.

Those who do not implement knowledge or do not exploit their talents remind me of what former United States President, Calvin Coolidge, said: *"Nothing in the world will take the place of persistence. Talent will not; nothing is more common than unsuccessful men with talent. Genius will not; unrewarded genius is almost a proverb. Education alone will not; the world is full of educated derelicts. Persistence and determination alone are omnipotent. The slogan 'press on' has solved and always will solve the problems of the human race."*

I would like to give the example of some of the sons and daughters of our beloved continent, Africa, who have exploited their talents in the field of literature and made us all proud to be Africans.

I will start with the Nigerian Writer, Poet and Playwright Wole Soyinka. He is the first African to win Nobel Prize in literature in 1986, followed by Najib Mahfuz of Egypt in 1988. Third is Ms Nadine Gordimer of South Africa in 1991. Fourth is J.M Coetzee of South Africa in 2003. They all made us proud.

One of the sons of South Sudan, Dr Peter Adwok Nyaba, published '*The Politics of Liberation Struggles in Southern Sudan: an Insider's View*' in 1997. This book won

Noma Prize in 1998. In 2000, a Northern Sudanese writer called, Leila Aboulela, won Caine Prize for African writing.

The prize was just founded in that year. It was won in the following years by young African writers (Helon Habila from Nigeria, 2001, Binyavanga Wainana from Kenya, 2002, Yvonne Adhiambo Owour of Kenya in 2003, this year it was won by Brian Chikwava from Zimbabwe)

Some South Sudanese writers/poets whose life has been between home and exile as a result of this political instability which has been going on for so long are; Taban Lo Liyong, Bona Malual Madut, Dr Francis Mading Deng, Sarah Modi, the late Es-Sir Annei, and Johnson Oliech (painter). At home we have Abel Alier, author of *Too Many Agreements Dishonoured.*

In the late 1980s up to 1990s we used to have Es-Sammani Lual and Al-Fatih Maluk plus some other young creative and active South Sudanese in the field of theatre in Khartoum. But because of the difficulties of life they left home for Western countries. I met these two gentlemen in Egypt in the 1990s before they left for resettlement. We need to think seriously about the future of drama in South Sudan.

While I was in Egypt, we used to have a group of young and enlightened South Sudanese who were very much concerned about the future of writing, painting, drawing and music in South Sudan. Some of us used to publish their works in Al-Khartoum and Al-Ittihadi Al-Dawliyah newspapers in Cairo.

They were the only two Sudanese newspapers which were published in Egypt. But I am told that they are not published any more. One may wonder what happens to talent such as was being portrayed in these two publications.

Some of the young writers/poets who were/are in Egypt include Arthur Gabriel Yak, Kon Madut Kon, Emmanuel Makur de Chagai, Bol Gak, Paul Achut, David Salah, Kidi Samuel, Abraham Madut Baak and Athieng Chol [female writer of short stories]. We also used to have some painters: Ma'nyang Musa Ma'ngok, David Oliver, Adau Deng Aguer,

Lusina Daniel Chol, Awaar Salvatore Lo'ngar, among others. Most of them have since migrated to Western countries due to hardships in Egypt.

Despite the difficulties of the liberation struggle, some efforts were made by the SPLM/A to establish theaters in some of the liberated areas. For example, a theatre was established by Daniel Kodi Angelo in Kapoeta County [Eastern Equatoria State, South Sudan] and another one was established by Fatiya Delga in Kaya town [Western Equatoria State] and another one in Yambio town [capital of Western Equatoria State] by Edward Abyei Lino. This was some years back when the war between the SPLA and the Government of the Sudan was at its peak.

Some years ago [2000-2001] when I was working with UNICEF/OLS on the Life Skills Educational Programmes for South Sudan, I met quite a number of young, creative and active South Sudanese painters; most of them were the former fighters of the Red Army of the SPLA who are generally known as *Jaysh Ahmar*. I worked with some of them as illustrators.

They include Peter Panchol, Chol Garang, Mareng Chuor, Joseph Garang and Majok Johnson. These painters and others whom I did not mention have a promising future if they take this talent seriously, develop it and get assisted. I would also like to remind any talented person that the bigger part of success lies in you.

As I mentioned earlier, these long years of war in our country have downplayed our creativity. We have been known by the international community for bloodshed, suffering, hunger, disease, poverty, displacement and refuge.

It is time now we show the world that we are also creative people. Much of our talents have not yet been discovered and therefore not exploited. Our oral literature has not yet been documented. It is through creativity only that we will put back Sudan in general and South Sudan in particular on the map of the world as a full active member of the international community.

It is important to provide the SPLA officers, soldiers and the civil population in South Sudan and the three conflict areas of Abyei, Southern Blue Nile and the Nuba Mountains with well-equipped libraries. Since our freedom fighters were provided with guns for the purpose of the liberation struggle and they did it well, it is also time to provide them with knowledge so that they face the challenges of rebuilding, development, progress and unity of our people with confidence. There is a need to care for *Jaysh Ahmar*. They are talented and patriotic. They are the seeds and the backbone of a strong, developed, peaceful, and progressive new Sudan.

We need to establish schools of arts and creative writing in five regions of new Sudan. We also need to establish theaters so that we entertain our freedom fighters who are being transformed from a situation of war to peace, where we need to nurture the principles of reconciliation, tolerance, unity and mutual understanding among our different tribes.

Remember music, dance, drama and other forms of art are good channels of communication, reconciliation and peace. NGOs would be even more appreciated if they could lend a hand of assistance to the talented people so that they develop their talents. These people also need a word of encouragement from the leadership of the new Sudan, so that they can reconstruct their creativity.

Some of the poets in the SPLA who fought with guns as well as with a pen are commanders: Pa'gan Amum, Edward Abyei Lino, Majak d'Agoot and late Yusuf Kuwa Makki, among others.

The message of writers/poets should always be humane: peace, equality, justice and unity of the people. As stated by the Nigerian writer Yemi D. Ogunyemi: "Today, writers are the ones best equipped to create and communicate the synthesis of ideas needed to solve the present predicaments, the world over.

They should continue (as peace-lovers) to articulate their imaginative and prophetic visions."

CREATIVITY LIVES ON IN SOUTH SUDAN

Sudan Mirror newspaper 1st-14th November, 2004

I talked about creativity in the previous issue, where I show-cased a number of gifted South Sudanese in the fields of writing, drawing, painting and theatre. This article is a continuation of the previous one.

I n the traditional life of South Sudanese, people used to express their sorrow, happiness, and love for a certain girl or social injustice through songs. And this is what Dr Francis Mading Deng has tried to show in his first book, *Tradition and Modernization: A Challenge for Law among the Dinka of the Sudan.*

For example, a singer in this song sang about his girlfriend Awut of whom he was to marry. These are the words of the song:

Because of Awut, I have become lean like a child

I say to my father

I have become lean because of Awut.

I am a man with a confounded mind

I do not know who to give the seat of my father

To go and sit on the bed,

I do not know who to give the bed of my father

Our words have ended with the times he would send me for water

And the times he would say, "Go and bring a mat from the byre"

I would bring them to my father

Is that not the value of a person's son?

People have confused us

I am like the son of a stranger

My father has tapped his chest in refusal

O clan of my father, shall I be only a tribesman?

In this song, the young man's father is dead, so here he is complaining to an elder against his uncle, whom he described in the song as his father. Deng translated this song from the Ngok Dinka Language of Abyei.

This book was first published in 1971 and won the Herskovits Award in the following year (1972). Dr Francis Mading Deng was born in his hometown, Abyei, in 1938. He attended schools in the South and the North as well.

He got a law degree from the University of Khartoum and went to the United Kingdom where he did a Masters Degree and then left for the United States of America where he obtained a Doctorate from the School of Law of Yale University in 1968.

Dr Deng served as Sudanese ambassador to Canada, the Scandinavian countries and the United States of America. Also, he was Sudan's state minister for foreign affairs. He is a senior fellow at the Brookings Institute, at the African Studies where he heads the branch of Foreign Policy Studies.

Dr Deng authored/ co-authored/edited more than 20 books in different fields, and they include: *War of Visions: Conflict of Identities in the Sudan, Sovereignty as Responsibility: Conflict Management in Africa* and two novels entitled, *'Cry of the Owl' and 'Seed of Redemption'*.

Dr Deng is the Representative of the United Nations Secretary-General for the Internally Displaced Persons Worldwide.

You have seen the role of songs in the experience of Dr Francis Mading Deng in his book I mentioned above.

Then with education, we discovered new ways of expression, such as novel, play, poetry and in this regard I would like to introduce to you a poem by the late commander

Yusuf Kuwa Makki, entitled,

My African-ness:

My mother,

With thousands of my apologies

Forgive me,

Forgive me for my frankness

For my courage.

Let me tell you,

Despite all the talk

About my Arabism

My religion,

My culture?

I am a Nuba

I am black

I am African.

African-ness is my identity

It is entrenched

In my appearance,

Engraved in my lips,

And manifested by my skin.

My African-ness

Is in the sound

Of my footsteps

It is in my bewildered past

And in the depth of my laughter.

Brothers,

Forgive me

For my frankness and courage

Despite my grandfather's humiliation,

Despite my grandmother's sale into slavery

Despite my ignorance

My backwardness

My naivety?

My tomorrow shall come.

I shall crown

My identity with knowledge

I shall light my candle

In its light

I shall build my civilization,

And at that time

I shall extend my hand,

I shall forgive those who tried

To destroy my identity

Because my aspirations

Are love and peace!

We observe from this poem that the poet had an open mind and open heart and the spirit of tolerance and forgiveness.

Late Yusuf Kuwa Makki was a teacher, poet and freedom fighter from the Nuba Mountains Region where he was its governor before he died.

He played a big role in encouraging the SPLA fighters in the Nuba Mountains to remain committed to their just cause and continue fighting amid the split in the movement in August 1991, when the then Government of Sudan cut the logistical routes from South Sudan to the Nuba Mountains and intensified its military operations against the SPLA in the region.

Commander Yusuf Kuwa Makki was the chairman of the SPLM/A First National Convention that was held in Chukudum, Eastern Equatoria State, South Sudan, in 1994.

Late Yusuf managed to draw attention of the international community to the Nuba Mountains. He had a number of unpublished poems. Commander Yusuf departed our world on 31 March 2001, after a long struggle with illness.

From the beautiful landscapes of the Nuba Mountains in western Sudan back to the beautiful jungle of South Sudan, where we will have a look at the experience of Victor Lugala,

with his poem entitled, 'Sweet Mother Juba'.

So here you are:

The Juba of yesterday

Is no longer the Juba of today:

The tarred road

That used to be sleek

Like snakes

Are craters

And the cars are in the mortuary.

When all roads led to Juba

Lorries hailed from Yei

Loaded with food supplies.

Cattle trecked many miles

From Bor and Terkeka townships,

And homes were noisy

With kids well fed.

Today food is a luxury

Eaten when you can afford.

People's hair has turned yellow

Because of malnutrition.

Where are the bars

That sold bottled beer

Like Skol, Dab and Bit Jenge?

The Juba night life

And the loud music

From Rejaf Night Club

Are a pleasant nostalgia.

The blaring of Congolese music

In home parties

Is replaced with dead silence

Imposed by the dusk-to-dawn curfew.

Juba has shrunk

Into a ghost town

Haunted by the enemy

Baying for the blood

Of the black people.

Victor Lugala is a poet and writer of short stories and journalist. He was forced by war to leave Yei and Juba for Northern Sudan, where he stayed in Khartoum and Port Sudan.

Eventually, he left Sudan for Tanzania to pursue his studies. After graduation, Victor came to Kenya and worked as editor for 'Hope' newsletter, published by the New Sudan Council of Churches.

Despite the long years that Victor spent in exile, his memories about those beautiful moments about Yei town, Rejaf, Atlabara and Kator Clubs in Juba are still present in his mind. Victor published his first collection of poems in Nairobi, Kenya in 2003. It is called *'Pot of Tears'*, which he dedicated to the women of South Sudan.

Victor Lugala is also a columnist with *The Sudan Mirror newspaper which is being published in Nairobi, Kenya by the Sudan Development Trust [SDT] and his column is entitled, 'Shoe-shiner'.*

Let us now see the experience of Edward Abyei Lino with his poem called, *The Mother:*

The ecstasy I yearn to live:

Meet my mother

Any time I live.

Having answered her calls

And concretized her dreams,

A free person, I say,

Like you and me…

Can thereafter fall very peacefully

Fully satisfied,

Deep into her soothing laps…

Pull her warm affection all over

As always flourishes

In every patriotic heart!

I see my mother

Every moment, every second

Resisting man-made sufferings,

Day and night supplicating:

When and from where

Shall the next meal and grace

For obedient children come.

So, rains instantly respond...

And our dear prosperous Land,

Having claimed many precious souls,

Graciously trickle her gifts...

Thus, shall we resist and exist!

This poem *'The Mother'* could be a metaphor,

representing our beloved country, Sudan. Actually, it is a long poem but I cut out the rest because of the space. Edward Abyei Lino was born in his hometown, the oil-rich region of Abyei, in 1946.

His traditional name is Abyei Wuor Abyei. And Abyei is a kind of a fig tree of which Abyei region was named after. And Abyei tree is widely found in Bahr Al-Ghazal and Upper Nile regions in South Sudan.

Abyei Area is defined as the territory of the nine Ngok Dinka Chiefdoms transferred by the British in 1905 from Bahr-al-Ghazal Province in South Sudan to Kordufan Province in western Sudan.

Edward Abyei Lino is a poet, freedom fighter and Commander in the SPLA. He has been writing poetry and involved in politics since the late 1960s when he was a student at the University of Khartoum.

The Government of Sudan's security men tore his two collections of poems to pieces when he was arrested in 1977. He released his first collection of poems in 2002, entitled,

'*Long Live the Monkeys*'. He has two unpublished collections of poems. Most of his poems are long epics.

It is to be-recalled that Edward Abyei Lino and late Yusuf Kuwa Makki were very close friends, and in fact, Edward dedicated his book, '*Long Live the Monkeys*' to him, martyrs and all the SPLA freedom fighters.

I will end this article with a book written by Dr Lual A. Deng. It is entitled, '*Rethinking African Development: Toward a Framework for Social Integration and Ecological Harmony*'.

The book is worth reading, especially, by the concerned people about the development in new Sudan during the six-year interim period [2005-2011].

The book addresses the issues of poverty reduction, economic reforms, environment degradations, democratization, civil strife and indebtedness. It was published on 1 November 1997, by Africa World Press.

SUDAN NEEDS UNITY IN DIVERSITY

Sudan Mirror newspaper-15th-28th November, 2004

As you all know, there is time for everything; there is time for birth and time for death, time for childhood and time for adulthood, there is time for suffering and time for joy and comfort, there is time for sadness and time for happiness, there is time for failure and time for success, there is time for war and time for peace.

So, it is now time for peace. After all, war is not the end by itself rather than a means of pressure for achieving an objective. The Bible says, "Happy are those who work for peace, God will call them His children."

There is no doubt that war is a bad thing and these are its consequences on the people: death, disability, displacement, refuge, lack of proper education, confusion, insecurity, misbehaviour, backwardness, sexual harassment, slavery, poverty, aggressiveness, hatred, dependency, lack of shelter, widowhood, separation, many orphans, lose of property, lose of dignity, culture loses some values, exploitation, name it.

We went through two destructive wars, the first civil war was waged by the Anyanya I [first southern liberation movement] under the Command of General Joseph Lago from 18 August 1955-1972 and the second civil war was waged by the SPLM/A from 16 May 1983 – present and it is being led by Colonel Dr John Garang de Mabior.

So many factors contributed to the break out of the two civil wars: Resources, political differences, racism, power, greediness, injustices, religious differences, selfishness, boundaries and ethnocentrism.

Whatever we try to do to solve all these differences, conflict will always be there, because it is part of life. But the most important thing is how it can be contained or how it can be managed when it arises.

We all know that Sudan is a multi-racial, multi-cultural, multi-religious, multi-lingual and multi-ethnic, and if at all there is going to be unity, it should be unity in diversity and not by imposing one of these on the rest.

As the two parties head to a comprehensive peace agreement, it is time now to reconcile with oneself, individuals, armed groups, clans, sections and with our different tribes. Reconciliation among our South Sudanese tribes is not only important but it is a must if we want to have a permanent peace in South Sudan.

South Sudanese know well how we lost so many precious lives because of tribalism. Therefore, South Sudanese should realize that there are so many challenges ahead upon the signing of the CPA. Tribalism is now the main enemy of the South Sudanese.

To me, southern Sudan went through two difficult stages; first civil war (1955-1972), second civil war (1983-present) and the third one is going to be the six-year interim period [2005-2011].

We need to take the stage of peace seriously the same way we took the wartime seriously. During peacetime we are going to have a war of visions and we have to prepare ourselves for that. And this is where the role of our educated elite and intellectuals comes in.

The present/future of South Sudan is in our hands and we can shape it the way we want for the betterment and well-being of our people who have been suffering throughout their lives. If the South Sudanese remain united during the interim period, and they must, they will be strong and therefore change the direction of Sudan for the better.

A united south Sudan will decide its fate after the end of the interim period with confidence whether it wants to remain united with the current Sudan or secedes.

We need to achieve and promote the virtues of peace, truth, mercy, justice and mutual understanding among ourselves. Also we need to promote human rights and the rule of law.

A peaceful South Sudan is a responsibility of all; traditional peacemakers, educated people, intellectuals, SPLM Party and the Government of Southern Sudan [GOSS]. All these elements should work hard to maintain peace and harmony so that people don't go back to war again. During war time we had/have war heroes. As we go to peace now, we will also need to have peace heroes. The faithful efforts by the international community to bring peace to Sudan should be appreciated by the Sudanese people in general and South Sudanese in particular. South Sudanese will get assisted by the international community as regard to development if they maintain peace and if there is transparency. The biggest responsibility to maintain peace is on the shoulder of Sudanese.

One of the factors that can keep South Sudanese united is if all South Sudanese who are either members of the SPLM or SPLA rally behind the SPLM Party as their only party during the whole interim period. But if the SPLM/A members join other parties then this will weaken the South Sudanese, GoSS and the SPLM/A.

Achieving a comprehensive peace agreement does not mean that all the South Sudanese who are members of the SPLM or SPLA can go back to all their former parties of which they were members before they joined the SPLM/A.

If they do so then the efforts of the years of the liberation struggle in the SPLA will go in vain. It is time you implement the principles and the objectives of the SPLM/A: creation of a new Sudan whose character should embody, justice, freedom, democracy and equality of which you fought for. What matters is not only you achieve your objective but also how you can maintain and preserve what you fight for and put it into practice.

Our last train will reach its last station when the six years finish. So if a comprehensive peace agreement is signed at any time from now, we will still have six stations ahead of us. It is not an easy journey.

Africa National Congress (ANC) in South Africa fought for so many years and eventually, it succeeded on its mission. It brought to an end the apartheid system and turned South Africa into a democratic country where whites and blacks could live together in harmony and peace.

The leadership of the ANC managed to maintain the unity of its people since 1994 when the country first turned into democracy, under the former president, Nelson Mandela. ANC is successful in its policy, concerning the unity of the people and this is because of its wise leadership that has established strong institutions and instilled in the people respect to the rule of law and human rights.

South Africans are now proud of the ANC, having brought them freedom, peace and national unity. They healed their wounds and reconciled among themselves when they achieved democracy. They celebrated 10 years of democracy and freedom this year.

Late Mwalimu Julius Kambarage Nyerere managed to unite Tanzanians. The unity of Tanzanians will always remain in the history as one of the greatest achievements of Nyerere. And Tanzanians up to now are being guided by the precious principles of peace, harmony and tolerance that were laid by Nyerere.

We have some experiences before us of great people worldwide who have worked for peace and harmony for their nations. Among them were Ghandi of India, Martin Luther King (Jr) of America and mother Teresa of Calcutta, India.

In the SPLM/A controlled areas, we have a traditional peace conference of Wunlit between the Nuer and the Dinka [communities]. It is a good step forward and it should be appreciated. That is why it is important for South Sudanese to unite. Because the unity of the south will not only affect it positively, but also Southern Blue Nile, the Nuba Mountains regions and Sudan as a whole.

We should all know that the culture of peace starts with and within the family. Therefore, it is a responsibility of the family to promote the culture of peace. If we are brought up in a family that appreciates and teaches the virtues of forgiveness, tolerance, harmony, democracy, equality and mutual understanding, then we can have a culture of peace.

By doing so, we will be building a healthy society. Because we all know that leaders are members of the society and the society is made up of individuals. Parents should be role models to their children. It is our responsibility to create a culture of peace and forgiveness among ourselves and with others too.

We also need to create a culture of appreciating other people's achievements. This will motivate him/her to make more achievements and after all it will be for the benefit of the nation and country. Any successful nation selects gifted people to occupy the key posts so that the rest can learn from them. It will be important for the new leadership of the Government of National Unity [GoNU in Khartoum] and the GoSS to build a culture of peace.

There should be an ongoing dialogue among the southerners (south – south dialogue) and intellectuals so that they create a culture of peace and forgiveness among southerners.

The interim period will be a big test for the SPLM/A, GoSS and South Sudanese intellectuals if they will keep committed to the virtues of justice, equality, peace, harmony and respect to other's cultures, language, human rights and the rule of law and a sense of responsibility.

There should be religious dialogue, Christianity with Islam, dialogue among the different denominations within Christianity in South Sudan. There should be respect to traditional beliefs (traditional religions). It would be wise if the Southern Sudanese Armed Groups could join the SPLA.

Otherwise, they have two choices, they either join the SPLA or the Sudan Armed Forces, but any third army can just complicate the situation. Also, the SPLM/A and the GoSS should care for the disabled, orphans and widows.

It is because of the struggle for these great virtues of freedom, peace, justice and respect to human rights and human dignity that they found themselves in such a situation. Equitable division of labour according to the specialization is needed.

Everybody should be involved in the development process. The GoSS should be concerned about the development of all the regions of the south equitably.

Distribution of chances of training and further studies equitably. It is important to establish institutions in the five regions of the new Sudan for peace building and conflict resolution. We need to build peace education clubs in all our schools. Promotion of traditional methods and conflict management is also important.

There is a need for us to have a national peace day. Writing articles on peace is needed. Presentation of lectures on peace and exchange programmes on our different cultures and heritage is also needed. There is a need for cultural festivals where people can be singing traditional peace songs. Religious institutions should play a big role in this issue and involvement of the youth is also important.

Holding workshops, seminars and conferences from time to time is needed. All media institutions (TV, radio, newspapers and magazines) should play a positive and instrumental role in promotion and building a culture of peace among our people. We should also see the experiences of other nations.

A CASE FOR THE CAPACITY OF SOUTH SUDANESE TO RULE THEMSELVES (1)

Sudan Mirror newspaper-Monday March 26th-Sunday April 8th, 2007

Pessimists everywhere and political manipulators in northern Sudan have often asked with a tongue in the cheek if South Sudanese can really rule themselves. Yes, South Sudanese have never known real political stability while peace has been an elusive commodity since 1955, all not of their own making.

This is when the first civil war erupted until 1972 when the Numayri regime signed a peace agreement known as the Addis Ababa Agreement. The agreement was signed with a southern liberation movement known as Anyanya I.

As the saying goes, the past informs the present and the future is in the womb of today. Accordingly, there are lessons to be learnt from history that influenced the situation in Sudan today.

The Anyanya I movement led by General Joseph Lago was fighting for the separation of southern Sudan from the north. The movement could not achieve its objective. Instead, southern Sudan got an autonomous status or a self-rule government for ten years during which southern Sudan witnessed a relative peace and stability that is until the Addis Ababa peace pact collapsed.

In the beginning of the 1980s the Numayri regime resorted to a policy of divide and rule in southern Sudan. Accordingly, the regime divided the southern region into three; namely, Bahr-al-Ghazal, Equatoria and Upper Nile regions.

The policy was adopted by successive regimes in Khartoum. Southerners who did not care about the well-being and welfare and unity of southern Sudan and their people were engaged as Khartoum's moles. Present day moles have similarly been recruited and the policy of divide and rule is subtle.

Reasons that led Southerners to rebel against Numayri's regime in 1983 were numerous. They ranged from social injustices, absence of equal representation of Southerners in the central governments in Khartoum to unfair distribution of the national wealth among others.

Incidentally, the Islamic laws that were introduced by the Numayri regime were not among the immediate reasons for the rebellion. This is because the war erupted in southern Sudan in earnest on 16 May 1983, while the Islamic laws that were known as 'September Laws' were introduced in September 1983. Dr Hasan Abdallah Al-Turabi, an Islamic Ideologue is believed to have been the architect of this policy.

The rebellion of Bor, Waat and Ayod [towns in Upper Nile Region in southern Sudan] were staged by 104 and 105 Battalions led by Major Kerobino Kuany-nyin Bol and Major William Nyuon Beny. It gave birth to the SPLM/A whose founding visionary was none other than the strategist Dr John Garang de Mabior.

Before the launching of Garang's movement in 1983, there was Abyei Liberation Movement/ Army (ALM/A) led by the late, Commander Luk Yowe, that came into being in 1981 and was transformed into Anyanya II after his death in 1982.

He died in action in one of the intensive battles against the Sudanese troops in Abyei Area. Later on, late Bagat Aguek and late Miokol Deng Majok [Miokol Deng Kuol] led the Anyanya II fighters in Abyei and Bahr-al-Ghazal regions to the military training centre in Bil-Fam (Bil-Pam), Ethiopia.

Before the arrival of the late Dr John Garang to Bil-Pam accompanied by Major Kerobino Kuany-nyin Bol, Major William Nyuon Beny, where SPLA recruits later on underwent military training, commanders Oyai Deng Ajak, Pa'gan Amum and the late Nacigak Nacialuk were already stationed there since 1982. Later on, Nacigak became a member of the SPLA Military High Command.

Southern Sudan experienced the first battles between the SPLA on one hand and southern separatists led by the late Akuot Atem Mayen, Samuel Gai Tut and William Abdallah Chuol on the other.

Those battles took SPLA five years (1983-1988) when their forces joined the SPLM/A. After the formation of the SPLM/A in 1983 the movement evolved a new vision for Sudan-which is the creation of a just, secular, democratic and united New Sudan.

From the start the SPLM/A embarked on identifying the root causes of the Sudan's problem. Dr Garang used to say that the so-called "The problem of the South is the creation of the successive central regimes in Khartoum". Hence, there was a need for the creation of a new Sudan on a new foundation, a new Sudan that recognizes the multi-cultural, multi-racial, multi-ethnic, multi-lingual and multi-religious reality of the country.

Thereafter, the movement called upon all the marginalized in the South, Nuba Mountains, Eastern Sudan, Darfur, Blue Nile and the far North to join the SPLM/A and struggle for the creation of a new Sudan that every Sudanese should be proud of.

As a result, the SPLM/A was joined by volunteer fighters from all walks of life and from different parts of Sudan. They included Muslims and Christians as well as those who believe in other African religions. As such the SPLM/A became a truly national movement, although many of the SPLA fighters hailed from South Sudan.

When the SPLM/A was launched the then President Ja'far Muhammad Numayri did not waste time to start undermining the liberation movement. He once commented ''Southerners are just going to behave themselves''. The liberation struggle went on and the Numayri regime left in 1985, then came General Su'war-al-Dahab and the government of the prime minister, Dr Al-Juzuli Daf'a-Allah, ruled the interim government for a year, then came the sectarian parties - Ummah Party and Democratic Unionist Party led by (Al-Imam) Al-Sadiq al-Mahdi and (Molana) Muhammed Uthman al-Marghani. In June 1989, they were overthrown by Brigadier-General Umar Hasan Ahmad al-Bashir in a military coup. They called their revolution 'National Salvation Revolution'.

Since the independence of Sudan on 1 January 1956, Sudan has witnessed three elective parliamentarian governments:

1-1954-1958;

2-1964-1969;

3-1986-1989

Sudan has also witnessed three military regimes:

1- 17 November 1958 - 21 October 1964, led by Ibrahim Abbdud;

2- 25 May 1969 - 6 April 1985 led by Ja'far Muhammad Numayri;

3- 30 June 1989-until 9 January 2005 (time of the signing of Sudan's CPA) led by President Umar Hasan Ahmad al-Bashir.

All these military regimes in Sudan seized power through military coups and all of them were Northerners. The reader can observe that the regimes were short-lived in power. And to answer the question above, can Southerners rule themselves? To me the answer is yes.

The period of twenty-one years that the late African Sudanese leader, intellectual, politician, agricultural-economist, academician and military strategist Commander Dr John Garang de Mabior spent in the bush leading the SPLM/A stands as evidence that Southerners are not only capable of leading themselves but the whole of Sudan.

Dr Garang was the only Sudanese leader who led the Sudanese people for a longer time in the history of Sudan. It is true that some prominent commanders such as Vice-President of the Government of Southern Sudan, HE Dr Riek Machar,

Sudan's Government of National Unity's (GONU) Foreign

Minister, HE Dr Lam Akol Ajawin, among others defected

from the mother movement (SPLM/A) during years of the

protracted war of the liberation struggle. **To be continued...**

A CASE FOR THE CAPACITY OF SOUTH SUDANESE TO RULE THEMSELVES (2)

Sudan Mirror newspaper-Monday 9th April-Sunday 22nd April, 2007

In the previous issue we examined the history of the Sudan since independence on 1 January 1956, the eruption of the southern rebellion on 18 August 1955, signing of the Addis Ababa Agreement in 1972 and the eruption of the second civil war in 1983 which led to the formation of the SPLM/A.

This is the last part. it is true that some prominent commanders such as the vice-president of the GoSS, HE Dr Riek Machar, Sudan's GoNU's Foreign Minister, HE Dr Lam Akol Ajawin, among others defected from the mother movement (SPLM/A) during the years of the protracted war of the liberation struggle.

However, the fact that they have come back to the mother movement is clear evidence that the future and destiny of South Sudan and Southerners lies in their unity.

Another evidence is that when the news of the mysterious death of the first vice-president and President of the GoSS, Cdr Dr.John Garang de Mabior, was announced some Northerners plus other members of the international community expected power struggle within the SPLM/A over who should take over the leadership of the movement forgetting the fact that the SPLM/A is a firmly grounded institution.

The prompt, efficient peaceful and smooth transfer of power to HE Commander Salva Kiir Mayardit surprised pessimists who were predicting doom for southern Sudan upon departure of Chairman Garang.

The differences of opinions between the SPLM party and some other southern political parties are normal in the world of politics.

In northern Sudan there are differences between the Democratic Unionist Party, Ummah Party, National Congress Party, Sudanese Communist Party, to mention but a few. So are differences of opinions between Hamas and Fatah in Palestine, Democratic Party and Republican Party in America, NARC-Kenya and ODM-Kenya in Kenya. These differences do not mean that the people of those countries cannot rule or govern themselves.

Throughout the years some of our Arab brothers in the north including the Islamic ideologue, Dr Hasan Abdallah al-Turabi, have been singing a song that Southerners cannot rule themselves. I one time watched Al-Turabi on Sudan TV saying that, "Southerners are a group of tribes that have nothing in common and if given an independent South Sudan they can just go kill themselves." He was expressing that while laughing.

These two years of the autonomous-GoSS have proven that Southerners are capable of running their own affairs and the affairs of the whole country (Sudan). Southerners should always aspire for the whole Sudan while they retain their right to self –determination after the six-year interim period.

It is good that we have a very strong document; CPA is binding and final. It cannot be amended nor can it be negotiated again. Because it has addressed the grievances of the marginalized Sudanese and it has also given them their rights.

Therefore, all the Sudanese especially the marginalized people of southern Sudan, three areas of the Nuba Mountains/Southern Kordufan, Blue Nile and Abyei region should hold the CPA document as their legitimate reference and defend it vigorously. Machakos Protocol which was signed on 20 July 2002 in Kenya has made the rights of the Sudanese people very clear.

The opening part concerning the state and religion says: "Recognizing that Sudan is a multi-cultural, multi-racial, multi-ethnic, multi-religious and multi-lingual country and confirming that religion shall not be used as a divisive factor, the Parties hereby agree as follows:

6.1 Religions, customs and beliefs are a source of moral strength and inspiration for the Sudanese people.

6.2 There shall be freedom of belief, worship and conscience for followers of all religions or beliefs or customs and no one shall be discriminated against on such grounds.

6.3 Eligibility for public office, including the presidency, public service and the enjoyment of all rights and duties shall be based on citizenship and not on religion, beliefs or customs." These articles from the Machakos Protocol show, among other things, that any person from the Nuba Mountains, Blue Nile, eastern Sudan, Darfur, central Sudan, southern Sudan- including Abyei and the people from the far north of Sudan, whether he/she is a Christian, Muslim or believes in one of the African religions, has full right to rule Sudan without preconditions.

Also, any Sudanese has full rights in Khartoum including Southerners, because that is our national capital. Besides, there is no reason why Southerners should give up their full legitimate rights in any part of Sudan, including Khartoum as 'Bilad al-Sudan', which is the current Sudan, means the 'land of the blacks'.

Southerners are among the rest of the African Sudanese of the Nuba, of the Mountains, Nubians of the far north, indigenous Africans in Darfur region of western Sudan, people of the Blue Nile in southeastern Sudan, and the Beja people of eastern Sudan.

Khartoum was also the headquarters of the Nilotic nationalities of the Shilluk, Nuer and Dinka but they, throughout the history of Sudan moved southward; following the River Nile till they settled in southern Sudan.

The Dinka, Nuer and Shilluk used to call Khartoum 'Kar-tuom' in their languages. Kar is a plural of Kiir which means river, and 'tuom' means to join or a juncture. So they called it that way because Khartoum is the juncture of the Blue and White Niles.

Africans such as Southerners, Darfurians, and the Nuba people among others have undisputable presence in Khartoum; that is why you get an estate called Wed-Nubawi [which means the son of Nuba] in Omdurman [Sudanese capital, Khartoum is made up of three towns; Khartoum, Khartoum North and Omdurman. They are all divided by the River Nile].

However, the legitimate right of the African Sudanese over Sudan does not give them a right to colonize the non-Africans (Arabs) who are in Sudan and became Sudanese when they take over power in Sudan through the 'intellectual revolution' that calls for the creation of a new Sudan.

This intellectual revolution is likely to succeed in the course of time if all the Sudanese intellectuals join hands and work hard for it. They can even make Khartoum, apart from being a political capital, an intellectual capital and pave the way for an intellectual revolution in the rest of Africa.

So to wrap up, the question now is not "can Southerners rule themselves?" The real question should be, "will the Northerners be able to rule themselves if the final results of the referendum of Southern Sudan after the end of the interim period turns out to be in favour of an independent South Sudan State?' This is because the factor that unites the North is the issue of southern Sudan.

GOSS AND SPLM NEED A NATIONAL PUBLIC BROADCASTER

Sudan Mirror newspaper, Monday 23 April-Sunday 6 May, 2007

The role of media in society is crucial. Accordingly one would have expected that by now, the GoSS, and SPLM as a political party would have endeavoured to set up media institutions.

This is not the case for over two years down the line since the signing of the CPA on 9 January 2005. It is true that there is Radio Juba and Southern Sudan TV in Juba; however, they neither cover the whole Sudan nor much of southern Sudan.

It is important to acknowledge that the media constitute the fourth power after the Executive (government), Legislature

(National Assembly) and the Judiciary. Media cannot therefore be ignored.

Sudan needs a national public broadcaster which apart from general dissemination of information would broadcast programmes on education, community development, modern farming techniques and animal husbandry. In a nutshell, they should be programmes for socio-economic development and the promotion of the rich Sudanese cultures.

As Sudan moves towards national census to be followed by mid-term elections and eventually Southern Sudan Referendum, what effective tool could be there for civic education which can reach millions of our people instantly than radio which broadcasts in key languages?

The same is the case for mobilization of potential returnees from northern towns and messages of hospitality for their smooth resettlements and reintegration into various communities.

It is no doubt the desire of SPLM to win the general elections all over Sudan which therefore requires that its campaign messages must reach all corners of the country; especially north, east and western Sudan.

Private broadcasting stations often do not bother with programmes on civic education, cultural and socio-economic development. They are commercial entities concerned with widening profit margins. As such their content tends to be controlled by advertisers.

On the other hand a public broadcaster is traditionally sustained by the state in the same manner as BBC and Voice of America (VOA) are sustained by their governments. Accordingly they are able to broadcast what would be considered as non-profitable programmes in public interest.

It may be argued that the cost of setting up a broadcasting station whose broadcasts can reach every corner of Sudan is high and should not therefore be a priority in view of many other development challenges. The stakes of not having one are equally high.

For instance, there have been complaints from Southerners that they cannot feel or see tangible peace dividends. Such complaints can lead to loss of faith in GoSS and SPLM which can be devastating at election time.

www.ingramcontent.com/pod-product-compliance
Lightning Source LLC
Chambersburg PA
CBHW060429290526
45791CB00002B/912